Emma and the Big Blue Summer

Written by Sharon Stamas

Illustrated by Wickie Rowland

BEAVER'S POND
PRESS

Edited by Laurie Herrmann
Illustrations by Wickie Rowland
Cover and interior design by Dan Pitts

ISBN: 978-1-64343-605-0
Library of Congress Number: 2023909443
Printed in Canada
First Edition: 2024

28 27 26 25 24   5 4 3 2 1

Beaver's Pond Press
939 Seventh Street West
Saint Paul, MN 55102
(952) 829-8818
www.BeaversPondPress.com

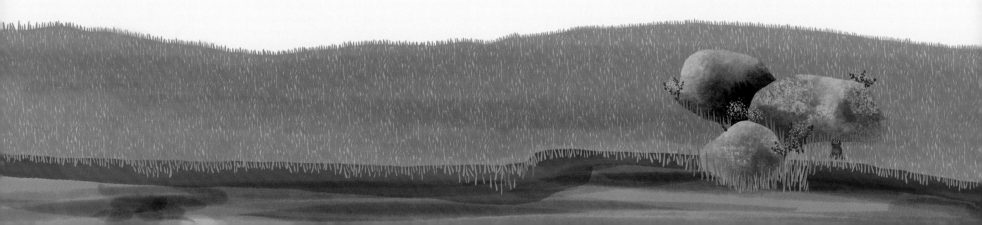

This book is
dedicated to Ezra.
Written for my dearest Riley.
Thank you, Lou.
—S.S.

To the nature lovers and the stories they bring us.
—W.R.

Emma was sad. It was 2020, and it was going to be the worst summer ever.

All Emma's big plans were canceled because of Covid-19. No Girl Scout camp, no time at the lake with her cousins, no nothing. Instead, Emma was stuck at her grandmother's house for the summer.

Emma loved Grandmother, of course.
Together, they made cookies, watched TV, and did puzzles.
But Emma was bored being inside all day long.

Grandmother had an idea.
"Emma, why don't you go to the pond? There's lots to explore there."

Emma shrugged. It was better than nothing.
Grandmother gave Emma a hug and sent her on her way.

The nearby pond was cool and quiet
in the summer breeze.

Emma could see little fish and tadpoles swimming,
but nothing too exciting.

Just then, Emma spotted a big blue heron on the other side of the pond. Standing on one leg, it seemed to be watching her.

"Hello," Emma said. The heron stretched his neck tall in response.

Emma sat at the edge of the water, half watching the fish and half watching the bird, who watched her right back.

When it neared suppertime, Emma waved goodbye to the heron and ran back to Grandmother's house.

That night, all Emma could talk about was the beautiful bird she'd met. She decided to call him Big Blue. She thought about the fish too and had an idea . . .

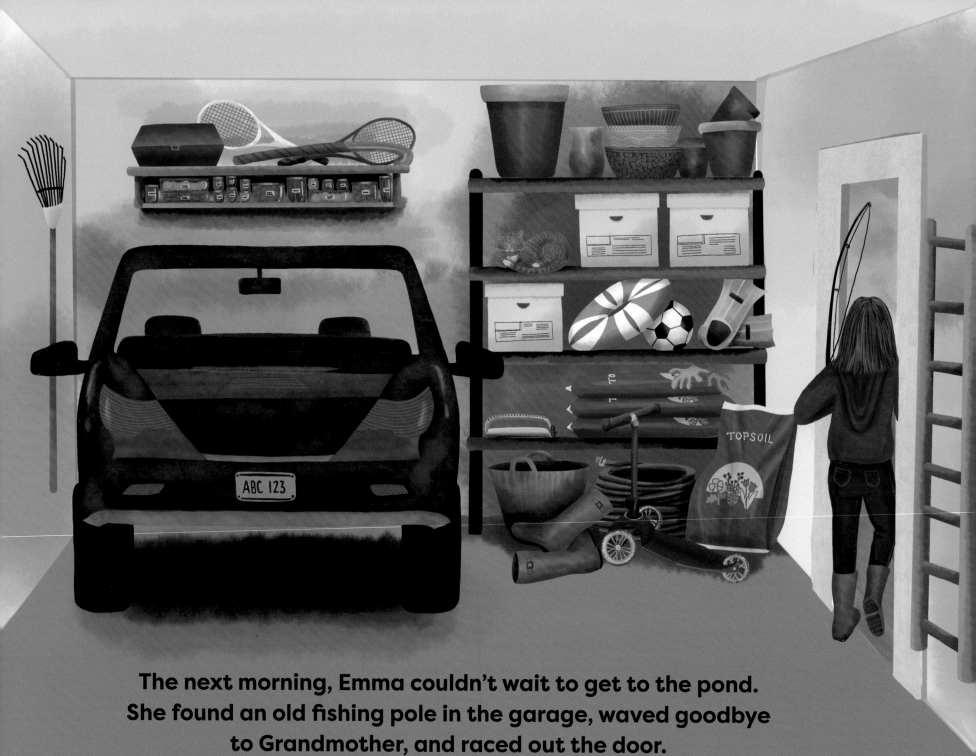

The next morning, Emma couldn't wait to get to the pond.
She found an old fishing pole in the garage, waved goodbye
to Grandmother, and raced out the door.

When she arrived, there was Big Blue, standing on Emma's side of the pond. Emma wanted to get closer. She took a few steps forward. Big Blue moved away from her, but not too far.

Emma stood on the bank of the pond
and cast her fishing line into the water.
Soon, she caught a fish.

"Here you go, Big Blue!" Emma said. She tossed the fish over to the heron, who, much to Emma's delight, cautiously picked it off the ground and ate it!

All summer long, Emma and Big Blue stuck together and became good friends.
Big Blue followed Emma around the pond, waiting for her to catch a fish.

When she did, Big Blue would come close so Emma could toss the fish to him.

He would pick it up in his long beak and gobble it down whole!

Sometimes, he would even catch the fish in midair!

Before Emma knew it, summer was over.
Emma hugged Grandmother and
gazed out at the pond where
Big Blue stood waiting for her.
Emma waved goodbye sadly.

Would she ever see him again?

Back at school, Emma thought about Big Blue.

Would he be warm enough in autumn?

Winter came, and Emma was still thinking about Big Blue.

When the pond froze over, where would he go?
Emma watched the snow fall and wished for summer.

When spring arrived, Emma took a special trip
to Grandmother's house. As soon as she could,
Emma raced to the pond, looking all around.

She saw leaves starting to grow, flowers starting to bloom.

And . . .

There, right where he had always stood, was Big Blue. He stretched his neck tall, as if to say, "Welcome back!"

Emma smiled. Now she knew that every year, as soon as winter was over, she and Big Blue would meet again at the pond.

What had started out as the worst summer ever turned out to be the most special summer of Emma's life!

About the Author:

From her porch overlooking a small pond during the first summer of Covid-19, Sharon witnessed a compelling bond of trust grow between a young girl and a great blue heron. Moved by the experience, she decided to write the story of Emma and Big Blue to share with her granddaughter.

Sharon, now retired, enjoyed careers in the medical and early childhood development fields. When not traveling, she and her husband, Lou, reside in Stratham, New Hampshire.

About the Illustrator:

Wickie Rowland is an award-winning author and illustrator from the Seacoast region of New Hampshire. She has been drawing her whole life and loves creating whimsical, meaningful worlds on the page—and in her garden! Her previous titles include *Good Morning, Strawbery Banke; Good Morning, Piscataqua; Finding Forget-Me-Nots: The Story of a Mindful Elephant;* and a meditative coloring book, *A Year in the Country.*

About the real Emma and Big Blue:

Here we have a snapshot of the real-life duo who inspired *Emma and the Big Blue Summer.* This photo was taken with permission from the young person and their family.